REVISITING TAIWAN'S DEFENSE STRATEGY

William S. Murray

China's recent military modernization has fundamentally altered Taiwan's security options. New Chinese submarines, advanced surface-to-air missiles, and, especially, short-range ballistic and land-attack cruise missiles have greatly reduced Taiwan's geographic advantage. Taipei can no longer expect to counter Chinese military strengths in a symmetrical manner, with Patriot interceptors, diesel submarines, surface warships, F-16 fighters, and P-3 maritime patrol aircraft. Taiwan must therefore rethink and redesign its defense strategy, emphasizing the asymmetrical advantage of being the defender, seeking to deny the People's Republic its strategic objectives rather than attempting to destroy its weapons systems. This would enable Taipei to deter more effectively Beijing's use of coercive force, would provide better means for Taiwan to resist Chinese attacks should deterrence fail, and would provide the United States additional time to determine whether intervening in a cross-strait conflict was in its own national interest. The strategy would also place the responsibility for Taiwan's defense squarely on its own military. Finally, it would restore the United States to unambiguous compliance with the Taiwan Relations Act.

The People's Republic of China (PRC) has been increasingly explicit about its military modernization objectives. China's 2004 white paper on national defense stated that "the PLA [People's Liberation Army] will . . . enhance the development of its operational strength with priority given to the Navy, Air Force and Second Artillery Force, and strengthen its comprehensive deterrence and warfighting capabilities."[1] The introduction of new classes of advanced surface warships; the unveiling of new nuclear-powered submarines, tactical fighter aircraft, and short- and medium-range ballistic missiles with advanced warheads; and an antisatellite demonstration—all attest to the determined pursuit of these goals.[2] Many analysts believe that China's near-term purposes are to deter Taiwan from declaring independence, to provide leverage by which to coerce a re-unification with Taiwan if deterrence fails, and to inhibit or delay U.S. intervention in such a conflict.[3]

Chinese employment strategies for these new weapons systems and potential capabilities remain unknown, though statements from senior leaders provide important hints. For example, President Hu Jintao is said to have stated in August 2007 that China had five major military priorities relative to Taiwan: establishing military readiness, conducting demonstrative exercises, "imposing a blockade on the Taiwan Strait," "carrying out combined firepower attacks," and "[conducting a] cross-sea landing."[4] Guo Boxiong, vice chairman of the Central Military Commission, boasted in March 2008, "We have the resolve and capability to deal with a major 'Taiwan independence' incident at any time."[5] The likely use of force would encompass three components: long-range precision bombardment, invasion, and blockade. These attack mechanisms would also likely be conducted in close coordination, not independently.[6] Taiwan faces the daunting challenge of how best to deny China the fulfillment of these objectives.

Previous studies of potential China-Taiwan conflict scenarios have concluded that Taiwan (either acting alone or with the assistance of the U.S. military) could defeat PRC coercion, thus presumably ensuring reliable deterrence.[7] Several of these studies have asserted that the Second Artillery (the PRC's strategic rocket force) possessed only a limited inventory of relatively inaccurate short-range missiles with which to attack Taiwan, restricting its role to what Robert Pape calls "coercion by punishment," terrorizing or inflicting pain on the population—a strategy that observers like Pape argue is rarely successful.[8] These circumstances, however, have now changed profoundly. Over the past decade China has greatly enhanced its capacity to "reach" Taiwan with far more accurate and decisive capabilities, and recent analyses question Taiwan's near-term ability to resist coercive force.[9]

For example, the PRC's expanding arsenal of increasingly accurate ballistic missiles can quickly, and with complete surprise, cripple or destroy high-value military assets, including aircraft on the ground and ships at piers. This emergent capability, plus the acquisition of long-range surface-to-air missiles (SAMs), suggests that the PRC has shifted its anti-Taiwan military strategy away from coercion by punishment toward denying Taiwan the use of its air force and navy.[10] Taiwan therefore faces a threat against which it has not adequately prepared and that offers the PRC a real prospect of achieving success before the United States could intervene. This is a very worrisome development.

Taiwan's responses to China's enhanced capabilities remain highly conflicted, a situation that reflects the deep political disagreements that shape Taipei's military policies. Taipei decreased its defense budgets in absolute and relative terms from 1993 until 2003, with only meager improvements thereafter.[11] These diminished efforts hardly seem commensurate with the increased threat that Taiwan confronts. They suggest either a state of denial about the threat, a gridlocked political system, misplaced faith in current systems and geographic advantages, or perhaps most disturbingly, a belief that the United States is certain to provide timely military assistance. Despite this ambivalence and its anemic defense budget, Taiwan has sought costly weapons systems from the United States, including PAC-3 (Patriot Advanced Capability, third version) missile systems, P-3 maritime patrol and F-16 fighter aircraft, *Kidd*-class destroyers, and diesel submarines. Taiwan is also reportedly attempting to develop offensive counterstrike capabilities indigenously, including the 360-mile-range Hsung-Feng IIE cruise missile.

Both approaches represent serious misperceptions of the threats posed to Taiwan and a misallocation of budgetary resources. The PAC-3s and other potential purchases are expensive, and they concentrate Taiwan's defense dollars on a limited range of capabilities that China is increasingly able to defeat. Offensive counterstrike weapons, furthermore, are potentially destabilizing, since China would have difficulty determining if such strikes originated from American or Taiwanese platforms. They are also unlikely to be acquired in numbers sufficient to deter China.[12]

More affordable, more effective, and less destabilizing means of defense against precision bombardment, invasion, and blockade are nonetheless available, but to take advantage of them, Taiwan must rethink its defense strategies. Rather than trying to destroy incoming ballistic missiles with costly PAC-3 SAMs, Taiwan should harden key facilities and build redundancies into critical infrastructure and processes so that it could absorb and survive a long-range precision bombardment.[13] Rather than relying on its navy and air force (neither of which is likely to survive such an attack) to destroy an invasion force, Taiwan should concentrate on development of a professional standing army armed with mobile, short-range, defensive weapons. To withstand a prolonged blockade, Taiwan should stockpile critical supplies and build infrastructure that would allow it to attend to the needs of its citizens unassisted for an extended period. Finally, Taiwan should eschew destabilizing offensive capabilities, which could include, in their extreme form, tactical nuclear weapons employed in a countervalue manner, or less alarmingly, long-range conventional weapons aimed against such iconic targets as the Three Gorges Dam.

Such shifts constitute a "porcupine strategy." They would offer Taiwan a way to resist PRC military coercion for weeks or months without presuming immediate U.S. intervention.[14] This shift in strategy might also be less provocative to the PRC than Taiwan's current policy of offensive defense. A porcupine strategy would enhance deterrence, in that a Taipei truly prepared to defend itself would be able to thwart a decapitation attempt—thereby discouraging Beijing from acting militarily. Perhaps most important, such a policy would allow the United States time to deliberate whether intervention was warranted. Washington could avoid a reflexive decision that would draw it into a war against a major power that had systematically prepared for just such a contingency for more than a decade.

This article has five principal parts. The first summarizes the history and rationale of the 2001 U.S. arms offer to Taiwan and explains why the weapons sales proposed are unsuited to the effective defense of the island. The second section outlines how China would probably attempt to destroy or neutralize the Taiwan air force and navy, and it proposes an alternative strategy for countering China's increasingly precise short-range ballistic missiles (SRBMs), cruise missiles, and manned tactical aircraft. The third part explores how Beijing's invasion options would change if Taipei lost its navy and the use of its air force. The fourth section examines PRC blockade options against Taiwan and suggests how Taiwan could more effectively deny China its blockade objectives. The concluding section considers the impediments to, and repercussions of, adoption by Taiwan of a "porcupine defense."

WHATEVER IT TAKES: THE 2001 U.S. ARMS SALE OFFER

In April 2001, reversing twenty years of American policy, the George W. Bush administration offered to provide to Taiwan eight diesel submarines for U.S. $12.3 billion.[15] This was part of a larger offer that also included six batteries of PAC-3 surface-to-air missiles for an additional $4.3 billion and twelve P-3C maritime patrol and antisubmarine aircraft at $1.6 billion.[16] This potential sale evoked predictably strong opposition from the mainland, stirred extensive internal Taiwanese debate, and brought significant American pressure on Taiwan to assent to these purchases.[17] For example, Richard Lawless, the Deputy Under Secretary of Defense for Asian and Pacific Affairs, stated that "the passage of this budget is a litmus test of Taiwan's commitment to its self-defense";[18] he also warned Taipei of "repercussions" if it failed to approve the arms purchase.[19]

One early version of the proposal also envisioned Taiwan buying new P-3Cs.[20] This would have required restarting a production line that had closed in 1990, at a cost of some $300 million per plane.[21] Many in Taiwan viewed the totality of this package as exorbitant.[22] Indeed, the leader of Taiwan's People First Party likened it to extortion by American mafiosi in exchange for protection from Chinese thugs.[23] The combination of high cost and intense divisiveness produced political theater and gridlock;[24] proposals to fund the package were defeated some sixty times between 2004 and 2007.[25] Six bitter years of stonewalling, stalemate, and wrangling finally ended in June 2007 with passage of watered-down legislation allocating a billion dollars to purchase rebuilt P-3 aircraft and upgrade Taiwan's existing SAM systems of the less advanced PAC-2 type, probably to PAC-3 standards.[26] The Legislative Yuan, however, allocated only about six million dollars to fund continued feasibility studies on the U.S. diesel submarine deal, thereby postponing or even killing it.[27]

The military rationale underlying the original arms package was one of a classic symmetrical response to perceived threats. Thus the P-3C Orion aircraft, which specialize in antisubmarine warfare (ASW) and open-ocean surveillance, could defend Taiwan from China's modernizing fleet of diesel and nuclear submarines. Similarly, eight modern diesel submarines would presumably defend against the PRC's increasingly impressive and capable surface forces and submarines. Finally, the PAC-3 would seemingly offer a viable defense for critical targets against Beijing's expanding inventory of short-range ballistic missiles, attack aircraft, and highly accurate land-attack cruise missiles.[28] Yet closer analysis suggests that none of these three weapons systems serve Taiwan's current or immediate future defense needs, that each would be acutely vulnerable to existing Chinese weapons and for Taipei would therefore be a major misallocation of resources. To support this conclusion I will review the presumed role of various potential capabilities in relation to the likely employment of Chinese capabilities.

PAC-2 and PAC-3 SAMs versus China's SRBMs

Taiwan clearly faces a major challenge in defending against Chinese short-range ballistic missiles. In 2005 Taiwan had an inventory of approximately two hundred earlier PAC-2 interceptors in three batteries.[29] Each PAC battery consists of a multifunction phased-array radar, an engagement control station, communications gear, and eight launchers with four missiles per launcher, plus one reload each. In theory, these three batteries of PAC-2 missiles could destroy up to 192 (that is, $3 \times 8 \times 4 \times 2$) Chinese SRBMs. SAM firing doctrine, however, mandates shooting two missiles against each target to increase the odds of success.[30] The downside of this enhanced kill probability is that it effectively halves the inventory of interceptors and doubles the cost of each attempted intercept. Unless Taiwan were to increase its inventory of PAC missiles hugely, it can expect to shoot down with the PAC-2 interceptors already in inventory at most ninety-six of the SRBMs targeted against it, or as many as 192 if Taipei upgrades all its current PAC-2 batteries to PAC-3 capabilities (which have sixteen missiles per launcher). Even this would allow over nine hundred of

China's 2007 inventory of a thousand SRBMs to arrive unchallenged at their targets.

Patriot interceptors are useless unless guided by the PAC radar. China could target these radars with SRBMs, cruise missiles, homing antiradiation missiles fired from tactical aircraft, or even Harpy antiradar drones launched from the mainland. Taiwan would then have to devote SAMs to defending the PAC radar, thus reducing the number available for defending airfields, leadership sites, critical infrastructure, or other key facilities.

Additionally, a PAC-3 installation protecting a particularly valuable target (e.g., Tsoying naval base) could be saturated and overwhelmed by large numbers of SRBMs. China could also initially fire older, less precise weapons to deplete Taiwan's inventory of interceptors, following them closely with unimpeded precision attacks using more accurate missiles. Mark Stokes, a close observer of China's Second Artillery, also notes that Beijing may have "a terminal guidance system that could preclude engagement by terminal missile defenses," such as Patriot interceptors.[31]

One argument commonly used to dismiss the threat posed by SRBMs is that the ballistic warheads lack the accuracy necessary for precision targeting. In a 2000 publication, for example, Michael O'Hanlon observed that the reported inaccuracy—a three-hundred-meter circular error probable (CEP)—of China's SRBMs made them little more than terror weapons.[32] However, O'Hanlon derived that estimate from 1999 and earlier sources; since then China has greatly improved the accuracy of its missiles, as well as the number in its inventory. Authoritative judgments are classified, but Thomas Christensen noted in 2001 that internal PLA sources assumed that the Second Artillery would be able to support accurate, concentrated attacks on enemy military assets.[33] *Jane's* in 2005 estimated China was producing ballistic missiles with CEPs of forty meters.[34] Mark Stokes wrote in 2006 that "at least 10 years ago, PRC missile engineers had been tasked to meet an accuracy requirement of below 50 meters circular error probability (CEP)."[35] Taiwan's Ministry of National Defense reported in September 2007 that China's SRBMs could strike within forty meters of their intended targets.[36] The Global Positioning System (GPS), which provides accuracy to within a few meters over most of the earth's surface, would be available to Beijing's weapons during all phases of launch and flight.[37] Further, the U.S. Navy's Office of Naval Intelligence also reported in 2004 that China is building ballistic missiles that can target large ships at sea; in 2006 it stated that these maneuvering warheads were guided by either infrared or radar seekers.[38] These reports reflect a growing consensus that China has mastered the engineering and manufacturing challenges involved in fielding highly accurate ballistic-missile warheads.

China's ballistic missiles are therefore no longer weapons for frightening populations but precision munitions. The Second Artillery's SRBMs provide the PLA the capability to destroy very large numbers of fixed targets with little or no warning.[39]

P-3s versus China's Submarines

Taiwan's purchase of P-3 Orion antisubmarine aircraft appears to make more sense. P-3s have a proven capability to find submarines; China has a large submarine fleet, over fifty diesel and nine or more nuclear submarines; and Taiwan's 1960s-vintage S-2 Tracker ASW aircraft is hopelessly obsolete.[40] Japan, another island state facing similar strategic imperatives, has up to 110 P-3s.[41] In reality, however, twelve P-3C aircraft will make little or no difference against China's submarine fleet. The reason is straightforward: P-3 aircraft require secure airfields from which to fly, but Taiwan will probably lose its airfields in the opening salvos of any all-out war with China. Air superiority will be doubtful. Further, a dozen P-3s can patrol only a fraction of the waters in which China's submarines could operate against Taiwan, and this fraction would be very likely reduced by combat losses. Twelve P-3s will have meaningful reconnaissance and maritime patrol roles to play during peacetime and scenarios of limited conflict, through their ability to conduct wide-area searches, but they will have little wartime utility.

Taiwan's Diesel Submarines versus the People's Liberation Army Navy

Diesel submarines can conduct effective operations against an opposing navy and merchant fleet, but only when they are used offensively. Admittedly, there are examples of diesel submarines effectively defending home or nearby waters. One is the Argentine Type 209 diesel submarine that operated against the Royal Navy during the 1982 Falklands War. Although making a number of attacks against surface and submarine contacts, it failed to damage any British ships. The Royal Navy, meanwhile, expended nearly its entire inventory of ASW weapons against the boat without sinking or disabling it.[42]

Conversely, there are many examples of effective employment of diesel submarines in offensive operations. The U.S., German, and British submarine forces have all excelled offensively. Yet technological developments after World War II dramatically altered the operational role of diesel submarines—they can no longer prowl for targets at relatively high speeds on the surface, submerging only to attack. Diesel submarines must now remain submerged, where their battery capacity forces them to hunt at low speeds—approximately four knots. They must also transit slowly to locations where enemy vessels might eventually deploy—geographic choke points, sea-lanes, and the waters around enemy harbors and naval bases being the most likely.

It is also erroneous to view diesel submarines as effective antisubmarine systems. A diesel submarine can, if equipped with appropriate torpedoes, attack another submarine, but modern submarines are very quiet and exceedingly difficult to detect. The Congressional Research Service, for example, reports that some Kilo-class diesel submarines are quieter than improved *Los Angeles*–class nuclear submarines.[43] This suggests that properly maintained, modern diesel submarines can be detected at ranges varying from two hundred yards to four nautical miles.[44] By maritime standards, these are very short distances. Diesel submarines, therefore, cannot reasonably expect to find other quiet submarines at long ranges.

Thus the importance of the low speeds of diesel submarines. If they can detect opponents only at ranges of a few miles, they will take a considerable amount of time to search large areas effectively. Furthermore, the hunting diesel submarine might well be itself detected and attacked by the hunted boat. Having no marked advantages in detection range, search speed, or quietness over opponents, diesel submarines cannot hope to become effective ASW platforms. Diesel submarines are therefore really specialists in antisurface warfare, mining, and intelligence gathering. These are all offensively oriented missions.

During a conflict, Taiwan would likely maximize the effectiveness of its submarines by either laying mines against Chinese ports or by attacking with torpedoes or cruise missiles warships leaving their bases. This would provide a much higher probability of success against People's Liberation Army Navy (PLAN) vessels than would the defensive tactic of waiting in or around Taiwanese waters for them. But China would have difficulty determining the origin of any resulting attacks and could attribute them to the United States, particularly any by Mark 48 torpedoes, which were included in the 2001 arms sale offer and a variant of which is carried by American submarines.[45] Such a contingency seems unnecessarily escalatory, especially since there are other, purely defensive and nonescalatory, alternatives that could more quickly offer Taiwan equal or better deterrence and at lesser cost.

TAIWAN'S VULNERABLE NAVY AND AIR FORCE
Taiwan's navy could probably fight the PLAN effectively. It possesses highly advanced equipment, including four *Kidd*-class destroyers and Harpoon antiship and SM-2 antiair missiles; its officers and men have a reputation for competence.[46] In consequence, China can be expected to look for a way to defeat this force decisively without a campaign of symmetrical, force-on-force attrition. A surprise, long-range, precision bombardment on Taipei's navy while it is in port seems a clear choice. Beijing would need sufficient weapon accuracy, availability,

and reliability, as well as targeting information, but all of these are now within the PRC's technical ability.

As mentioned above, problems of accuracy that used to characterize Beijing's long-range weapons have likely been solved. Accurate weaponry is useless without knowledge of the precise location of targets, but targeting Taiwan's surface combatants in port is increasingly easy. In the age of Google Earth, the latitude and longitude of naval piers at Tsoying, Suau, and Taiwan's other naval bases are easy to determine exactly, and these piers are finite in number. Moreover, many of Taiwan's naval bases are also commercial ports, suggesting that direct observation of surface ships within them would be a simple matter. Ships in port rarely shift berths, so Beijing could readily monitor the location of most, if not all, of Taiwan's surface combatants in port on a day-to-day basis.[47]

If Beijing knew that Taipei's destroyers were tied up to a given pier, it could readily program cruise or ballistic missiles to strike the appropriate aim points. Even if jamming denies GPS and similar signals, technology like laser radar guidance allows automatic target recognition.[48] Deficiencies in accuracy can also be compensated for by submunitions, which can damage targets within a larger area. China has developed ballistic-missile-deployed submunitions since at least 2000.[49] Submunitions designed to penetrate and damage runways, which China has almost certainly developed for its SRBMs, would also be highly effective against moored naval vessels.[50]

Unclassified information regarding China's weapons-system reliability is not available. But technological shortfalls no longer plague China's space program or significantly retard its ability to manufacture dependable high-technology consumer products such as memory chips, digital processors, digital cameras, cell phones, or personal computers. China thus seems increasingly capable of achieving adequate weapons-system reliability. Producing sufficient numbers of weapons is also well within the PRC's technical and budgetary capacities. Devoting, say, a hundred SRBMs to the destruction or crippling of Taiwan's navy would likely be a fruitful allocation of China's inventory of precision weapons.

Taiwan's air force is also threatened by long-range precision bombardment, but by different means.[51] The Taiwan air force has nine air bases, from which approximately 145 F-16, fifty-six Mirage 2000, and 131 F-CK-1A Indigenous Defense Fighters operate.[52] An examination of the air bases using Google Earth shows upward of four hundred protected revetments at these nine bases, approximately half of them covered and perhaps hardened.[53] This gives credence to the reports of underground hangars at Ta-Shan Air Base in Hualien that reportedly can protect over half of Taiwan's tactical fighter aircraft. Other underground shelters exist at Taitung Air Base and perhaps elsewhere.[54] The table describes results of open-source satellite imagery examination of Taiwan's air bases.

TAIWAN'S AIR BASES

Air Base	Latitude/ Longitude	Runways (Taxi)	Runway Length × Width (ft)*	Warheads	Shelters	Revetments	Tunnels
Taoyuan	250319/ 1211431	1 (1)	10,015 × 145	8	41	46	0
Hsinchu	244905/ 1205621	1 (2)	11,955 × 148	12	43	11	0
Ta-Shan	240148/ 1213629	1 (1)	7,959 × 140	5	0	0	8
Chashan	240109/ 1213652	1 (2)	9,022 × 148	8	23	10	0
Chiayi	232747/ 1202329	2 (1)	10,007 × 148 5,307 × 74	9	34	37	0
Tainan	225700/ 1201220	2 (1)	10,007 × 148 10,007 × 148	8	43	50	0
Kangshan	224657/ 1201553	2 (1)	8,019 × 145 7,435 × 145	6	4	0	0
Ching Chuan Kang	241525/ 1203738	1 (2)	12,000 × 148	12	31	16	0
Taitung	241104/ 1203914	1 (1)	11,055 × 147	8	29	0	12
Sungshan	250353/ 1213303	1 (1)	8,578 × 197	5	0	0	0
Makung	243409/ 1193747	1 (1)	9,843 × 148	8	4	8	0
Total		14 (14)		89	252	178	20

* Nearly all runway data in this table are taken from posted airport information on Google Earth. Information not provided was determined using Google Earth.

Any Chinese attempt to destroy individual aircraft in hardened shelters would be hindered by the large number of targets. The Second Artillery might have to devote at least one highly accurate unitary warhead to each covered aircraft revetment. This allocation of over two hundred missiles could be wasted, however, if Taiwan did not place any aircraft in these revetments but instead parked them in the open to defeat such targeting. Such dispersed aircraft, however, would be vulnerable to SRBM-delivered fragmenting submunitions. This too would be an inefficient use of a potentially large percentage of the Second Artillery's short-range ballistic missiles, and neither method would threaten any aircraft protected in underground shelters.

A better option for the Chinese would be to target the runways with warheads designed to crater them and so prevent Taiwan's aircraft from taking off.[55] For example, a loaded F-16 apparently requires approximately 2,500 feet of uninterrupted runway to take off; U.S. doctrine, however, demands a fifty-by-five-thousand-foot minimum operating strip for tactical aircraft operations.[56] Taiwan's air bases have fourteen runways ranging from 5,307 to 11,995 feet long, and these strips are on average approximately 150 feet wide. If China's SRBMs are sufficiently accurate and reliable, six unitary warheads each creating a fifty-foot crater could cut a 12,000-by-148-foot runway into six segments, each smaller than a U.S. minimum operating strip.[57] Where taxiways could also serve as runways, they would also have to be cratered. Using this logic, China would have to devote at least eighty-nine perfectly accurate warheads (see the "warheads" column of the table) to Taiwan's runways and taxiways to prevent their use by tactical aircraft. The PRC cannot rely on 100 percent SRBM reliability and accuracy, but something between a hundred and two hundred unitary warheads could deny Taiwan the use of its air bases for a while. This number would be greater if accuracy and reliability were poor and ballistic missile defenses were effective; conversely, it could be smaller if China has runway-penetrating submunitions, tactical aircraft or cruise missiles can reliably deliver antirunway munitions, or fighter aircraft require longer takeoff or landing distances than assumed.[58]

China has reportedly acquired runway-penetrating bombs from Russian sources.[59] It also seems likely that the Second Artillery has developed rocket-delivered warheads. A Google Earth image at 40°29'20" north latitude, 93°30'02" east longitude, depicts what is likely Chinese testing of a concrete-penetrating submunition warhead. Mark Stokes asserts that in fact the Second Artillery already has runway-penetrating submunitions, terminally guided.[60] In any case, there is little reason to doubt that China has developed suitably accurate antirunway weapons to support such a campaign as envisioned here. As a point in evidence, Taiwan recognizes that its runways present a critical vulnerability and has acquired the ability to repair them rapidly under combat conditions.[61] Disturbingly, however, as late as 2007 at least one Taiwan airfield's runway repair capabilities consisted of "a pile of gravel and pile of sand at the apex of the runways. Both piles were uncovered, exposed to the elements, and obviously had been very long in place; furthermore, there was no earthmoving equipment stored anywhere near the piles."[62] Effective rapid runway repair during sustained ballistic missile strikes requires highly trained and motivated teams. If Taiwan has established and maintained such teams, it should be able to keep some of its airfields operable. Observers might be forgiven doubts, however, given other manning problems that afflict Taiwan's military.[63]

Among those problems is a shortage of pilots. For nearly a decade Taiwan has struggled to maintain a ratio of one pilot to one modern fighter aircraft. Bernard

Cole relates that Taiwan's minister of defense has seriously considered mothballing some of its Mirage 2000s in an effort to increase the pilot-to-plane ratio.[64] Attrition among pilots by any means would be a very serious matter.

Finally, Taiwan has on at least two occasions conducted exercises in which tactical aircraft flew from highways.[65] Yet this expedient incurs a host of logistics problems, very low sortie rates, and increased vulnerabilities to traditional, fifth-column, or PRC special operations forces attacks.[66]

The key point is simple and sobering: the Second Artillery's expanding inventory of increasingly accurate SRBMs probably allows Beijing to incapacitate much of Taiwan's navy and to ground or destroy large portions of the air force in a surprise missile assault and follow-on barrages.

An Invitation to Invasion?

Hypothetical Chinese invasion fleets have always been presumed to risk devastation by Taipei's highly regarded air force. Yet even if Taiwan's fighters could take to the air and conduct coordinated defensive operations after suffering a long-range precision bombardment, they would still have to prevail against the Chinese air force and navy's growing inventory of fourth-generation Su-27, Su-30, J-10, and J-11 aircraft, all with impressive antiair capabilities. Other mortal threats include Beijing's four (soon to be eight) batteries firing the land-based S-300 PMU2 surface-to-air missile, which with its 120-mile range can reach nearly across the Strait of Taiwan and make penetration of China's airspace "difficult if not impossible" with F-16s and F-15s.[67] This difficulty could be exacerbated by the ninety-mile SA-20, which China is sending to sea on its pair of Luzhou-class destroyers, and by the fifty-four-mile HHQ-9 SAMs on both of its Luyang II destroyers.[68] Combined, these weapons systems could effectively defend an invasion fleet against any tactical aircraft that got airborne.

It is also widely assessed that Beijing lacks the amphibious lift required to conduct a successful invasion. A spate of recent mainland amphibious-ship construction, however, suggests that Beijing continues to pursue that option. The launching and outfitting of the Yazhou-class landing ship (LPD) in 2006 and 2007 at Shanghai's Hudong shipyard means that shortly an invasion fleet would have helicopter and air-cushion-vehicle support.[69] An additional invasion capability will be gained if China acquires from Russia the sixty-knot *Zubr*-class amphibious hovercraft, which can carry three main battle tanks, ten armored personnel carriers, or 140 troops. Long-swirling rumors of the impending sale of six or more are gaining credibility.[70] Further, the ten Yuting-II tank landing ships built during 2003 and 2004 increased China's inventory of that type by approximately 50 percent.[71] The total number of amphibious vessels required to support a Taiwan invasion is debated; it depends on attrition rates, weather, loading and unloading times, the use of civilian shipping, availability of off-loading infrastructure in Taiwan, Taiwan's will to resist, and other factors both physical and subjective.[72] Regardless, it is apparent that China has not forsaken an invasion option and has the ability to develop rapidly additional amphibious forces.

Rethinking Taiwan's Defenses

Taiwan can do little to prevent a Chinese bombardment by many hundreds, even thousands, of precision-guided munitions. Taipei might have a better payoff, therefore, in seeking not to defeat the incoming warheads but to prevent the attack from achieving its objectives. For instance, one technologically unsophisticated and relatively affordable measure would be to harden key civil and military facilities—burying them or constructing concrete shelters that can withstand multiple direct hits.[73] This would be especially important for civilian leadership facilities, military command posts, and communications systems. It could even be done for Taiwan's three Patriot interceptor sites, which, Google Earth reveals, are in the open. Keeping the launchers and radars in caves or hardened bunkers would cause Beijing to devote more warheads to them. Also, having survived the initial bombardment, the launchers could be rolled out to protect against follow-on harassment strikes by SRBMs, cruise missiles, and tactical aircraft.

The same logic would further suggest redundancy of critical infrastructure—such as food and water distribution systems, medical services, wartime command and control, warning radars, or civil defense information networks. However, Taiwan's electrical grid is particularly vulnerable. For example, the magnitude 7.6 earthquake that struck central Taiwan on 21 September 1999 resulted in a complete loss of electricity in the northern half of the island. A major cause was heavy damage to the Chungliao electrical substation, "a major hub in the island's high voltage transmission network that directs 45% of the north's power demand."[74] Attacks on this attractive target could be resisted either by distribution redundancy or emergency generators (with fuel) to supply vital networks and facilities during and after a bombardment. Tax incentives or building-code revisions could help create such capacity.[75]

As a further example, Taiwan could complicate China's targeting. Decoys are an excellent and affordable way to do so. In 1999 Serbia reportedly misled many NATO precision-guided munitions with such primitive ruses as simulated tanks made of wood and tarpaulins.[76] Taiwan could complicate Beijing's targeting options with radar emitters that seduce homing antiradiation missiles, inflatable "missile launchers," and the like. Properly done, these measures could cause the Second Artillery to waste a large percentage of its warheads on false targets.

Another worthwhile alternative to trying to shoot down ballistic warheads would be making critical targets mobile. Fixed targets are relatively easy to locate and destroy with precision weaponry (unless buried or hardened), but mobile targets are not, as the United States discovered in its unsuccessful hunt for Scuds in the Iraqi western desert during the first Gulf War.[77] An option would be for Taiwan to move its Patriot radars frequently between several sites. For its part, the navy could consider frequently shifting its ships' berths, increasing the time they spend at sea, or even anchoring them in its ports, especially in time of heightened tensions.[78] Another option would be hardened pens for missile patrol craft, in which they might survive an initial SRBM attack.[79] Taipei could also rotate its fighters between airfields or between hardened shelters, in a high-stakes analogy to three-card monte. Future weapons acquisitions could emphasize mobility and concealment.

Beijing's short-range ballistic missiles are highly accurate, but they are not infinite in either destructive power or number.[80] In the face of such passive defenses they might well fail, however many struck targets, to achieve the true purpose for which they were fired—destruction of Taiwan's ability, or willingness, to resist "regime change."

Under existing conditions, however, a surprise long-range precision bombardment would likely cost Taiwan its ability to fly useful numbers of tactical aircraft in a coordinated manner or to sortie its navy. This prospect has important implications. For one, it suggests that additional tactical fixed-wing aircraft requiring long runways would not be a wise investment. If their mission would be countering invasion and (more important) preventing the PRC from using its own aircraft in a bombardment, invasion, or blockade, Taiwan would do better to invest more in mobile SAM systems. For instance, Taiwan reportedly has 162 medium-range Improved Hawk missiles but as few as five launchers.[81] The surface-launched advanced medium-range air-to-air missile (SLAMRAAM), a truck-mounted version of the highly capable AIM-120 AMRAAM, if acquired and integrated with existing systems, would significantly enhance Taiwan's antiair capability.[82] Taiwan could enhance its short-range man-portable and truck-mounted air-defense systems, such as the Stinger, Avenger (a truck-borne Stinger), and Chaparral; they might be stored in hardened or disguised shelters and frequently moved between them. These steps would greatly complicate targeting and help deny China air superiority in the aftermath of a major bombardment. On this view, further investments in fixed-site surface-to-air missiles, such as Taiwan's silo-based Sky Bow 1, would seem unwise due to their vulnerability to precision-guided munitions, unless they can withstand multiple direct hits.

REPELLING AN INVASION

An all-out Chinese campaign to topple the Taiwan government might combine bombardment with invasion. If Taiwan's navy and air force were neutralized or destroyed by the bombardment, the army would have to repulse or defeat an invasion alone. There are several weapons—all affordable and unambiguously defensive in nature—that, if purchased, could greatly improve its chances of doing so.

At the top of this list are mobile coastal-defense cruise missiles (CDCMs), such as truck-mounted Harpoons. A fairly small number of these missiles would likely devastate China's armor-carrying amphibious shipping, which would have to come well within range, and then stop, to disembark the vehicles. Recent naval history strongly suggests that a vessel loaded with tanks or armored personnel carriers could be sunk or put out of action by a single five-hundred-pound (or lighter) high-explosive warhead, such as cruise missiles deliver.[83] Thus far, no Chinese amphibious vessel has a robust anti–cruise missile capability.[84] Cruise missiles' targets could be acquired by mobile radars.[85] Best of all, CDCMs could greatly enhance Taiwan's ability to destroy an invasion force without third-party assistance.[86]

A second class of weaponry that would be highly effective in repelling an invasion comprises attack helicopters, such as the Apache AH-64D. Taiwan, recognizing the utility of helicopters, has sixty-three AH-1A Super Cobras and has set in motion an initiative to buy thirty Apaches in 2008 from the United States for an estimated U.S. $2.26 billion.[87] These aircraft would be highly effective against armor that approached in landing craft or got ashore, if adequately protected during the preparatory bombardment. Additionally, helicopters' ability to fly low affords a degree of immunity to long-range surface-to-air missiles.

The Multiple Launch Rocket System (MLRS) is another truck-mounted weapon that might be appropriate for Taiwan. These mobile launchers could be readily hidden or sheltered. Equipped with appropriate rockets, their long-range precision fire could greatly weaken any PLA toeholds.[88] They might do so even if key bridges or roads were impassable; a handful of MLRS sites could cover the entire island. Advanced tanks, artillery, and antitank weapons should not be left off this list of effective hardware, but Taiwan already has sizable stocks of most of them.

Another hardware recommendation, less strictly associated with ground warfare, involves surf-zone sea mines. These weapons, designed for waters less than ten feet deep, are extraordinarily difficult to counter and would bedevil the planning or execution of any Chinese invasion of Taiwan. A former commandant of the U.S. Marine Corps, General James L. Jones, stated in 2002 that "the inability to clear mines from the surf zone is the 'Achilles' heel of our maneuver force.'"[89] U.S. Navy mine warfare officers also attest to their effectiveness and to the speed and ease of deploying them.[90] Since they are lightweight and portable, shallow-water mines can be quickly and easily moved from secure bunkers to where they are needed. They are also quite inexpensive, relative to many of the other weapons systems Taiwan might choose.

None of these weapons would be effective if Taiwan's army were not highly trained or motivated. Unfortunately, however, its conscript ground forces reportedly "suffer from low morale, a poor NCO [noncommissioned officer] program and poorly maintained equipment."[91] Also, Taiwan's reserve forces are very weak; conscripts serve only fourteen months before entering the reserves.[92] In any case, conscript-based armies are poorly suited to the high-technology combat that would characterize an invasion attempt by the PRC. These problems are no doubt rooted in structural, social, and political issues beyond the scope of this article. However, it should be pointed out briefly that the aim of thwarting the ultimate objectives of a PRC attack (or better, thereby discouraging Beijing from the attempt) would be best served by an all-volunteer, highly professional and highly trained army. An all-volunteer army, though consistent with the stated desires of many elected officials, could not be developed quickly.[93] It would increase personnel costs, but it would also increase the ground force's deterrent value, since it would reduce the likelihood of total collapse at the beginning of hostilities, which numerous informed observers believe is a real possibility.[94]

WITHSTANDING A BLOCKADE

If Taiwan's military and leadership were to ride out a bombardment and repel an invasion, China might then consider an extended blockade designed to prevent Taiwan from importing energy.[95] The Republic of China would be acutely vulnerable to such an action, since it imports over 98 percent of its energy requirements. All these fuels pass through easily identifiable bottlenecks, including off-loading terminals and processing locations that would be susceptible to destruction or mining.[96] Imported energy is also carried on easily identifiable ship types, which could be isolated, diverted, or even sunk. Additionally, Taiwan's refiners are required only to maintain crude oil stocks equivalent to thirty days' demand.[97] This all suggests that an energy blockade's effects would be felt very quickly throughout Taiwan, and could be severe.

One wonders how long Taipei could resist Beijing's demands under such conditions. It is equally unclear how a blockade that was preceded by a long-range precision bombardment could be countered, whatever defensive military options Taiwan pursues. A partial solution might lie in the civil, rather than military, sphere. Specifically, Taiwan could prepare for a blockade by stockpiling critical energy, food, and medical supplies and planning for rationing and financial contingencies.[98] Such preparations would reassure Taiwan's leadership and citizenry that they could withstand a blockade, thus reducing the likelihood of panic and early capitulation. A second objective of comprehensive preparations and plans would be to delay significantly the point when shortages would force Taipei to concede.[99]

Perhaps most important, the United States could use the interim to deliberate how best to respond. For instance, Washington could withhold the possibility of intervention as leverage to induce Taipei to behave within acceptable parameters, both before and during crises. With the luxury of time, the United States might find ways to assist that avoided direct military conflict with China—for example, supplying critical military material via airlift, much as the Nixon administration did for Israel during the 1973 Yom Kippur War, or by shipping oil to Taiwan on reflagged, escorted tankers. The United States might, conversely, decide to intervene with conventional force in an overwhelming but carefully phased manner that took advantage of asymmetrical American advantages. A standing realization by China that it could well be defeated in such a contingency would significantly contribute to deterrence.

THE PORCUPINE REPUBLIC

It is difficult to escape the conclusion that China either already has or shortly will have the ability to ground or destroy Taiwan's air force and eliminate the navy at a time of its own choosing. This prospect fundamentally alters Taiwan's defense needs and makes the intended acquisition from the United States of diesel submarines, P-3 aircraft, and PAC-3 interceptors ill advised.

Diesel submarines are poor antisubmarine platforms, since with their low speed and limited underwater endurance they simply cannot search quickly large volumes of ocean for quiet submarines. These physical restrictions also limit their versatility as antisurface platforms. They are, for all practical purposes, four-knot minefields. At a cost of over U.S. $1.5 billion each and with indeterminate delivery dates, conventional submarines also carry significant opportunity costs, as some in Taipei clearly recognize. Finally, submarines are no more likely than other naval ships tied up at exposed piers to survive the opening salvo of a war with China.

Taiwan's apparent decision to purchase up to twelve submarine-hunting P-3C aircraft is similarly brought into question. Although these planes can collect valuable information during peacetime and in crisis, in wartime they would be sitting ducks while on the ground (though hardened shelters might protect P-3s) and aloft would require uncontested air superiority to have any chance of accomplishing their mission.[100] In any case, Taipei cannot protect its runways. Patriot surface-to-air missiles have some utility against short-range ballistic missiles, but China already has the means to defeat this expensive air-defense system.

The implication is that Taiwan would be far better served by hardening, and building redundancy into, its civil and military infrastructure and systems. In that way the island could reasonably hope to survive an initial precision bombardment, deny the PRC the uncontested use of the air, repel an invasion, and defy the effects of a blockade for an extended period. Many of these actions, in fact, would be consistent with recent efforts by Taiwan to improve its defenses. Others, however, would entail substantial shifts that some in Taiwan's navy and air force would doubtless oppose. Air force leaders would be understandably loath to admit that their fighters cannot defend Taiwan's skies; their navy counterparts might similarly resist suggestions that their fleet is acutely vulnerable in port. Both services' political champions would certainly challenge the implications of this article's analysis. So too would the arms manufacturers who stand to benefit from the sale of aircraft, ships, and supporting systems to Taiwan.

Yet under present conditions it is doubtful that the people and government of Taiwan could withstand a determined PRC assault for long. A hasty American military intervention would be Taiwan's only hope, but only at the risk of strategic miscalculation and nuclear escalation. A "porcupine" strategy—a Taiwan that was patently useless to attack—would obviate the need; it would also make a determined Taipei conspicuously able to deny the objective of a bombardment or defeat an invasion, thus deterring either scenario. Ability to resist a full-scale campaign—long-range precision bombardment, invasion, and blockade—for a substantial amount of time would allow its potential allies to shape their responses carefully. Above all, demonstrable Taiwanese resilience would diminish Beijing's prior confidence in success, strengthen cross-strait deterrence, and reduce the risk of the United States being dragged into a conflict with China.[101]

Meanwhile, a porcupine strategy would restore the United States to unequivocal adherence to the Taiwan Relations Act, since Taiwan would be in the market only for defensive systems. Taiwan would find itself with a better defense for fewer dollars, and the United States would abide by the 17 August 1982 joint communiqué declaring that it would "not exceed, either in qualitative or in quantitative terms, the level of those [arms] supplied in recent years . . . and that it intends gradually to reduce its sale of arms to Taiwan, leading, over a period of time, to a final resolution."[102]

Finally, and most important, a porcupine approach would shift the responsibility for Taiwan's defense to Taiwan, rendering U.S. intervention in a cross-strait battle a last resort instead of the first response. Many observers believe that Taiwan today relies unduly on a perceived American security guarantee and does not do enough to provide for its own defense. Yet since 2000 the Kuomintang and the Democratic People's Party have not framed a defense debate that could produce the open, honest appraisal that is desperately needed if domestic consensus on a viable defense is to be achieved. A Taiwan that China perceived could be attacked and damaged but not defeated, at least without unacceptably high costs and risks, would enjoy better relations with the United States and neutralize the threat posed by many of China's recently acquired military capabilities. Unfortunately, political gridlock in Taipei stands in the way of any such hopes. It is not that Taiwan does not do enough to construct a viable defense but that it is not doing the right things.

NOTES

The views expressed in this article are those of the author and do not necessarily reflect those of the U.S. Navy, Department of Defense, or government. The author gratefully acknowledges the major contributions of Craig Koerner and thanks Jonathan Pollack; Bernard Cole; Rear Adm. Michael McDevitt, USN (Ret.); Lyle Goldstein; Michael Chase; Marshall Hoyler; Andrew Erickson; and Christopher Weuve for their invaluable suggestions.

1. *China's National Defense in 2004,* available at www.fas.org/. China's 2006 defense white paper did not emphasize the same point.

2. Many of these improvements have been proudly displayed on the Internet. See, for example, the intelligently moderated China Defense Forum at forum.china-defense.com/. The annual U.S. Department of Defense reports to Congress on the "Military Power of the People's Republic of China" also chronicle many of Beijing's military developments.

3. U.S. Defense Dept., *Annual Report to Congress: Military Power of the People's Republic of China 2007* (Washington, D.C.: 23 May 2007), p. 15, available at www.defenselink.mil; Roger Cliff et al., *Entering the Dragon's Lair: Chinese Antiaccess Strategies and Their Implications for the United States* (Santa Monica, Calif.:

RAND, 2007), available at www.rand.org; Ron O'Rourke, *China Naval Modernization: Implications for U.S. Navy Capabilities—Background and Issues for Congress* (Washington, D.C.: Congressional Research Service [hereafter CRS], 20 July 2007).

4. Wang Yu-yen, "Hu Jintao Says the Only Task of the CPC Armed Forces Is to Launch War against Taiwan," *Lien-Ho Pao,* 27 August 2007, Open Source Center [hereafter OSC] CPP20070827312001.

5. Wang Shibin, "Guo Boxiong Sets Out PLA Tasks, Warns 'Taiwan Independence' Forces," *Jiefangjun Bao,* 7 March 2008, p. 1, OSC CPP20080307710003.

6. Thus, in all probability, an invasion or a blockade would be preceded by a long-range precision bombardment. These scenarios could, and likely would, involve extensive information warfare operations, as well as "decapitation attacks," in which senior political and military leaders would be personally targeted, perhaps by assassins or precision-guided munitions.

7. See, for example, Michael O'Hanlon, "Why China Cannot Conquer Taiwan," *International Security* 25, no. 2 (Fall 2000), pp. 51–86; Michael A. Glosny, "Strangulation

from the Sea? A PRC Submarine Blockade of Taiwan," *International Security* 28, no. 4 (Spring 2000), pp. 125–60; Robert S. Ross, "Navigating the Taiwan Strait: Deterrence, Escalation Dominance, and U.S.-China Relations," *International Security* 27, no. 2 (Fall 2002), pp. 48–85; and David A. Shlapak, David T. Orletsky, and Barry A. Wilson, *Dire Strait? Military Aspects of the China-Taiwan Confrontation and Options for U.S. Policy* (Santa Monica, Calif.: RAND, 2000). However, these studies were published before the evidence of PLA modernization was fully apparent.

8. Robert A. Pape, *Bombing to Win* (Ithaca, N.Y.: Cornell Univ. Press, 1996), pp. 12–26.

9. See, for example, Thomas J. Christensen, "Posing Problems without Catching Up: China's Rise and Challenges for U.S. Security Policy," *International Security* 25, no. 4 (Spring 2001), pp. 5–40; and Lyle Goldstein and William Murray, "Undersea Dragons: China's Maturing Submarine Force," *International Security* 28, no. 4 (Spring 2004), pp. 161–96. For a careful, and rather discouraging, analysis of Taiwan's security situation see Bernard D. Cole, *Taiwan's Security: History and Prospects* (London: Routledge, 2006).

10. Pape refers to this use of bombardment as "coercion by denial," maintaining that such strategies are much more likely to succeed than strategies that rely on punishment; *Bombing to Win*, pp. 27–35.

11. For details see Shirley Kan, *Taiwan: Major U.S. Arms Sales since 1990*, CRS Report for Congress (Washington, D.C.: CRS, 5 July 2005), pp. 17–22.

12. A thoughtful criticism of such offensive systems is provided by Denny Roy, "Taiwan Perilously Ponders Its Strategic Missile Force," Jamestown Foundation *China Brief* 6, no. 20, available at jamestown.org/china_brief.

13. A PAC-3 interceptor costs approximately $3.2 million. Rich Chang, "PAC-3s Will Protect Taiwan, MND Says," *Taipei Times*, 21 March 2005, p. 3, available at www .taipeitimes.com. Although the cost of Chinese SRBMs is not publicly available, the fact that the PRC is building over a hundred a year suggests they are much more affordable to the PRC than are PAC-3 interceptors to Taiwan.

14. This would align with the 11 September 2007 speech by Thomas J. Christensen, Deputy Assistant Secretary of State for East Asian and Pacific Affairs, to a U.S.-Taiwan Business Council defense industry conference. Christensen said that the United States desires a "strong and moderate Taiwan . . . that maintains the military capacity to withstand coercion for an extended period of time"; available at www.state.gov. Further, section 3302 of the Taiwan Relations Act states, "The President and the Congress shall determine, in accordance with constitutional processes, appropriate action by the US in response to any such danger" (usinfo.state.gov/eap). Such process would likely take a significant period of time.

15. Ross, "Navigating the Taiwan Strait," p. 82.

16. Jim Wolf, "Taiwan Submarine Builder Not Chosen Yet: Envoy," Reuters, 29 September 2004; prices are in U.S. 2001 dollars. The complete package offered in response to a Taiwanese request also included "54 Mark-48 torpedoes, 44 Harpoon submarine-launched anti-ship cruise missiles, 144 M109A6 Paladin self-propelled howitzers, 54 AAV7A1 amphibious assault vehicles, AN/ALE-50 electronic countermeasure systems for F-16s, and 12 MH-53 mine-sweeping helicopters"; Kan, *Taiwan*, p. 6. Kan's excellent report contains a comprehensive accounting of the arms sale's subsequent tortuous progress.

17. See, for example, "China Opposed to US Submarine Sale to Taiwan: FM Spokeswoman," *People's Daily*, 21 November 2001, available at english.peopledaily.com.cn.

18. Nicholas Kralev, "Election Results Threaten U.S. Arms Agreement," *Washington Times*, 16 December 2004, p. 17.

19. "U.S. Official Warns of 'Repercussions' If Taiwan Fails to Approve Weapons Deal," Associated Press, 6 October 2004, available at taiwansecurity.org. Other public pressure from the United States included statements by Stephen Young, the director of the American Institute of Taiwan, who called frequently on Taiwan to fund the package. See Rich Chang, "Time Expiring on Arms Deal: Congressman," *Taipei Times*, 23 February 2006, p. 2, available at www.taipeitimes.com; and Jane Rickards, "Taiwan Rejects Most of U.S. Arms Package Offered in 2001,"

Washington Post, 16 June 2007. Peter Rodman, Assistant Secretary of Defense for International Security Affairs, testified in 2004 to Congress, "We expect Taiwan to go forward with its plan to pass a 'Special Budget' this summer to fund essential missile defense and anti-submarine warfare systems and programs"; Kan, *Taiwan,* p. 20, citing statement before the House International Relations Committee, *The Taiwan Relations Act: The Next 25 Years,* 108th Cong., 2nd sess., 21 April 2004, note 102.

20. Lu Chao-lung, "US Demands Exorbitant Price for Purchase of Submarines, Anti-submarine Planes," *Chung-Kuo Shih-Pao,* 8 May 2003, Foreign Broadcast Information Service [hereafter FBIS] CPP20030508000022.

21. *Jane's Defence Weekly,* 21 May 2003.

22. In comparison, the Russians in 2002 sold eight Project 636M Kilo-class submarines to the PRC for a reported $1.6 billion. See, for example, "Sevmachpredpriyatiye Enterprise Ready to Construct Submarines for Chinese Navy," Agentstvo Voyennykh Novostey, 3 September 2002, FBIS CEP20020903000123. All eight Kilos were delivered to China by the end of 2006.

23. "Warning on Arms Purchase Angers Taipei Opposition," Reuters, 7 October 2004, available at taiwansecurity.org.

24. Taiwan's defense minister, Lee Jye, for example, said, "I have said I will resign if the budget is not passed. I am serious"; "Defense Minister Threatens to Quit over Sub Budget," *Taipei Times,* 15 June 2004, p. 4, available at www.taipeitimes.com.

25. Ted Galen Carpenter, "Taiwan's Free Ride on U.S. Defense," *Asian Wall Street Journal,* 23 April 2007, available at www.cato.org.

26. Taiwan apparently decided to buy twelve P-3Cs; Reuters, "U.S. May Sell Weapons to Taiwan," *New York Times,* 13 September 2007.

27. Shih Shiu-chuan, "Legislature Finally Passes US Arms Budget," *Taipei Times,* 16 June 2007, p. 1, available at www.taipeitimes.com.

28. "By November 2007, the PLA had deployed between 990 and 1070 CSS-6 and CSS-7 short-range ballistic missiles (SRBM) to garrisons opposite Taiwan. It is increasing the size of this force at a rate of more than 100 missiles per year, including variants of these missiles with improved ranges, accuracies, and payloads"; U.S. Defense Dept., *Annual Report to Congress: Military Power of the People's Republic of China 2008* (Washington, D.C.: 29 February 2008), p. 2. The 2008 DoD report states (pp. 2, 56) that China has up to 250 DH-10 land-attack cruise missiles. *Jane's* claims a ten-meter-CEP accuracy for these weapons; "China Tests New Land-Attack Cruise Missile," *Jane's Missiles and Rockets,* 1 October 2004, available at www.Janes.com. CEP is the radius of a circle within which a *warhead* will land at least 50 percent of the time.

29. Chang, "PAC-3s Will Protect Taiwan, MND Says," p. 3.

30. A Taiwan Ministry of National Defense official leaked that PAC-3 interceptors have a 0.8 probability of kill; Chang, "PAC-3s Will Protect Taiwan, MND Says." By extension, they also have a probability of miss of 0.2. The probability of at least one of a pair of PAC-3 interceptors striking their target would therefore be $1 - (0.2 \times 0.2) = 0.96$.

31. Mark A. Stokes, prepared statement before the U.S.-China Economic and Security Review Commission, *China's Military Modernization and Export Controls Hearings,* 109th Cong., 2nd sess., 16 March 2006, p. 44, available at www.uscc.gov/hearings/2006hearings/transcripts.

32. O'Hanlon, "Why China Cannot Conquer Taiwan," p. 58.

33. Christensen, "Posing Problems without Catching Up," p. 26.

34. John Hill, "Missile Race Heightens Tension across the Taiwan Strait," *Jane's Intelligence Review,* 1 January 2005. This article also reports the Chinese development of land-attack cruise missiles with ten-meter accuracy.

35. Stokes, prepared statement before the U.S.-China Economic and Security Review Commission, p. 44.

36. "Chinese Missiles Aimed at Taiwan Exceeds [*sic*] 900," *China Post,* 11 September 2007, available at www.chinapost.com.tw. A 2007 Taiwan article claims newer SRBMs have a CEP of thirty, or even twenty, meters; see Cheng Ta-ch'eng, "Taiwan Report on PRC Missile Threat to World," *Taipei*

Lu-chun Yueh-k'an, 26 January 2007, OSC CPP20070524312005. Cheng does not provide a source for this estimate in his otherwise well-documented article.

37. Russia's GLONASS system, which would presumably be available even if the U.S. GPS were denied, provides similar accuracies, as will the even more accurate Galileo system, to be built by the European Union and China. China is also putting into orbit its Beidou navigation satellite system.

38. Scott Bray, Office of Naval Intelligence Public Affairs Office, "Seapower Questions on the Chinese Submarine Force," e-mail to author, 6 March 2007.

39. Stokes relates that "2nd artillery doctrine stresses surprise and disarming first strikes to gain the initiative in the opening phase of a conflict"; Stokes, prepared statement before the U.S.-China Economic and Security Review Commission, p. 44.

40. One close observer's assessment to the author was, "I don't think any of the S-2s are operable."

41. See "P-3C Orion Maritime Patrol and Anti-submarine Warfare Aircraft, USA," *Air Force Technology,* www.airforce-technology.com. Japan obtained and honed this significant force during the Cold War to oppose the threat posed by the Soviet submarine force. The multimission capability of these aircraft, however, justifies their continued operation by Japan and other countries, including the United States.

42. Adm. Harry D. Train, USN, "An Analysis of the Falkland/Malvinas Islands Campaign," *Naval War College Review* 41, no. 1 (Winter 1988), p. 40.

43. Shirley Kan, Christopher Bolkom, and Ronald O'Rourke, *China's Foreign Conventional Arms Acquisitions: Background and Analysis,* CRS Report for Congress (Washington, D.C.: CRS, 10 October 2000), p. 61, available at www.fas.org. China has twelve Kilo submarines.

44. See figure A6-6 in Tom Stefanick, *Strategic Antisubmarine Warfare and Naval Strategy* (Lexington, Ky.: Institute for Defense and Disarmament Studies, 1987), p. 278. Stefanick concludes that a *Los Angeles*–class submarine can be detected at ranges from one to twenty-five nautical miles. If a Kilo-class diesel submarine is quieter than an improved *Los Angeles*–class unit, which in turn must be quieter than an unimproved *Los Angeles,* then Stefanick's graph suggests that detection ranges for a Kilo are on par with those of *Ohio*-class SSBNs.

45. Kan, *Taiwan,* p. 6.

46. Taiwan also has nine *Chi Yang* (ex-U.S. *Knox*-class) frigates, eight *Cheung Kung*–class frigates that are copies of the U.S. *Oliver Hazard Perry* class, six frigates of the *Kang Ting (Lafayette)* class, and some fifty missile patrol craft. See Cole, *Taiwan's Security,* pp. 119–34.

47. Ship movements in port would require the interruption of daily training and maintenance, involve several harbor tugs, and complicate the planning of harbor operations. As a result, it is somewhat expensive and generally avoided.

48. See, for example, "Laser Radar (LADAR) Guidance System," at the Israeli Aerospace Industry's *Defense Update: International, Online Defense Magazine,* www.defense-update .com/products/l/ladar.htm. I make no claim that the PRC has this technology but only observe that high weapons-system accuracy is no longer a monopoly of the United States.

49. Bruce Bennett, "The Emerging Ballistic Missile Threat: Global and Regional Ramifications," in *Emerging Threats, Force Structures, and the Role of Air Power in Korea,* ed. Natalie W. Crawford and Chung-in Moon (Santa Monica, Calif.: RAND, 2000), p. 193.

50. The technology for such weapons is not cutting-edge. The British JP233, used in the Gulf War, for example, was an aircraft-delivered anti-airfield munition that dropped thirty 34 kg cratering bomblets and 215 2.4 kg anti-personnel mines. The bomblets had two stages—the first used a shaped charge to blow a hole in the concrete runway into which the second stage would fall, exploding to create a large crater. The antipersonnel mines were sufficiently strong and sensitive to disable heavy equipment passing nearby, slowing runway repair. The JP233 weighed approximately 1,587 kg; see "JP233," *Wikipedia,* en.wikipedia.org/wiki/JP233. Germany's STABO runway-penetrating submunitions weigh just 16 kg each. China's CSS-7 SRBM is thought to be able to carry 800 kg warheads

at least 174 miles, which suggests that in terms of mass delivered, two SRBMs could create the same airfield damage as a single JP233. Similarly, a single CSS-7 could also carry approximately the mass of forty-eight STABOs, though its ability to carry that much volume is uncertain. See "CSS-7," Missilethreat.com (Claremont Institute).

51. An informed discussion of this idea can be found in Lt. Cdr. William E. Bunn, USN, "Shock and Awe with Chinese Characteristics," *Chinese Military Update* 3, no. 2 (March 2006). Readers who type "Hualien" into Google Earth can observe for themselves the location of the hardened aircraft revetments at Taiwan's Chashan and connected Ta-Shan air bases.

52. See "Republic of China Air Force (ROCAF)," TaiwanAirPower.org; and Cole, *Taiwan's Security*, pp. 105–18. Cole points out that Taiwan also has ninety or more F-5 aircraft but notes that these largely obsolete aircraft are used mostly for pilot training.

53. Knowledgeable individuals who have inspected Taiwan's aircraft shelters have observed to the author that they are "inadequate in coverage and strength."

54. Oliver August, "Secret World That Guards Taiwan," *London Times*, 23 May 2001. Google Earth images of Taitung's underground shelters, which are approximately two thousand feet long in total, suggest that they can protect a substantial number of aircraft.

55. This is apparently consistent with at least some Chinese operational concepts. See the discussion in Cliff et al., *Entering the Dragon's Lair*, pp. 62, 81–109.

56. See U.S. Air Force Dept., "Mission Planning," *Pilot Operating Procedures: F-16*, Multi-Command Instruction 11-F16, sec. 2.2.2, 21 April 1995, available at www.fas.org. Despite this, in U.S. doctrine the minimum operating strip for flight operations is fifteen meters wide and 1,525 meters long (or fifty by five thousand feet). This additional length is more important during landings than on takeoff. See "Aviation Facilities," *Federation of American Scientists*, www.fas.org.

57. Cole reports a Taiwanese Ministry of National Defense estimate that a 500 kg unitary warhead from an SRBM would create in a runway a crater ten meters deep and twenty wide. *Taiwan's Security*, p. 113.

58. A 1999 RAND study estimated that dozens of missiles with nonpenetrating submunitions bomblets could attack a U.S. air base effectively; John Stillion and David Orletsky, *Airbase Vulnerability to Conventional Cruise-Missile and Ballistic-Missile Attacks* (Santa Monica, Calif.: RAND, 1999), pp. xiii, 13, 14. I contend that runway-penetrating submunitions further reduce that number.

59. "KAB-500Kr TV-Guided Bomb," SinoDefence.com.

60. "These warheads include things like, for example, submunitions, terminally guided submunitions for example, for runway cratering in order to pin down an air force on the ground or to disrupt naval operations"; Stokes, prepared statement before the U.S.-China Economic and Security Review Commission, p. 42.

61. The Washington, D.C., company Rapid Mat U.S. was awarded a $43 million contract in 2002 to provide rapid-runway-repair kits to Taiwan by the end of 2004. See the U.S. Defense Dept., Press Release 145-2, 22 March 2002, available at www.defenselink.mil/contracts. The company's website, www.coltrapidmat.com, lists the materials used in rapid-runway-repair kits.

62. E-mail to the author from a knowledgeable individual who visited the base.

63. See, for example, Cole, *Taiwan's Security*, pp. 74–78, 89–90, 102, and 111–12.

64. Ibid., pp. 111–12.

65. This occurred in 2007 and in 2004. See "Planes Land on Highway as Taiwan Simulates Attack from Rival China," *China Post*, 15 May 2007, available at www.chinapost.com.tw; and "Taiwan Turns Highway into Flyway," Associated Press, 22 July 2004, available at taiwansecurity.org.

66. Shlapak, Orletsky, and Wilson, *Dire Strait?* p. 33.

67. For a description of the threat posed by advanced Russian SAMs see John A. Tirpak, "The Double-Digit SAMs," *Air Force Magazine Online* 84, no. 6 (June 2001), www.afa.org/magazine. The quoted phrase is that of Lt. Gen. Bruce Wright, USAF, in Eric

Talmadge, "While U.S. Is Bogged Down in Iraq China Seen Making Big Military Strides," *Japan Times,* 1 October 2007, available at search.japantimes.co.jp.

68. "SA-N-6/20 'Grumble' (S-300 Fort/Rif)," *Jane's Strategic Weapon Systems,* 29 December 2006, available at www.Janes.com; and U.S. Defense Dept., *Annual Report to Congress: Military Power of the People's Republic of China 2006* (Washington, D.C.: May 2006), p. 5.

69. See Richard D. Fisher, "Chinese Aspects of Singapore's IMDEX Naval Technology Show," *International Assessment and Strategy Center,* 20 June 2007, available at www.strategycenter.net.

70. See, for example, "China Orders 6 Giant Russian 'Zubr' Hovercraft," *Defense Industry Daily,* 13 September 2007, available at www.defenseindustrydaily.com.

71. "Yuting-II Class (LSTH)," *Jane's Fighting Ships,* 29 January 2007, available at www.Janes.com.

72. O'Hanlon's discussion in "Why China Cannot Conquer Taiwan" of the difficulties facing an invasion of Taiwan is still quite good, although his conclusion regarding the survivability of Taiwan's air force during bombardment has been overcome by developments.

73. James Mulvenon has been making this point since at least 2000. Steven Mufson, "U.S. Faces a Dilemma on Taiwan: Warship Sale Could Fuel China Tensions," *Washington Post,* 14 April 2000, available at taiwansecurity.org. A hardened aircraft shelter in Europe cost approximately four million dollars in 1999; see Stillion and Orletsky, *Airbase Vulnerability to Conventional Cruise-Missile and Ballistic-Missile Attacks,* p. 31. Shlapak, Orletsky, and Wilson strongly advocate hardening not only aircraft revetments but also air base fuel-tank farms, fuel distribution systems, and critical maintenance facilities; *Dire Strait?* pp. 32–33. Bernard Cole too argues strongly that Taiwan should harden critical facilities, in *Taiwan's Security,* pp. 113–14.

74. Restoration of power to northern Taiwan businesses and residences took weeks. Risk Management Solutions, *Event Report Chi-Chi, Taiwan Earthquake* (n.d.), pp.

13–15, available at www.rms.com/publications/Taiwan_Event.pdf.

75. Although this would be a significant commitment, it is not entirely without precedent. Israeli law mandates that all new houses have a "safe room" designed to withstand a bomb blast.

76. "And Now, the War Forecast," *Economist Technology Quarterly,* 17 September 2005, p. 23.

77. The United States reportedly dedicated nearly 2,500 missions to finding and destroying Scuds, with no successes. Mark Thompson, "The Great SCUD Hunt," *Time,* 15 December 2002, available at www.time.com.

78. Because an anchored ship swings, or pivots, around its anchor, it cannot be struck by warheads aimed at coordinates. It could be hit, however, by area-covering submunitions or guided warheads, perhaps from antiship cruise missiles, to which China has devoted much effort.

79. Missile craft sheltered in facilities modeled on Germany's famously impervious submarine shelters in Brest, France, during World War II would be vulnerable to cruise missiles, however, or to the effects of thermobaric warheads, which could be delivered via missiles or aircraft. See Jonathan Marcus, "Analysis: How Thermobaric Bombs Work," *BBC News,* 4 March 2002, available at news.bbc.co.uk.

80. Milošević withstood the destruction caused by 6,728 U.S. precision-guided munitions striking approximately six thousand aim points before conceding to demands. Taiwan, with an island's additional defensive characteristics, ought to be able to do even better. See Benjamin S. Lambeth, *NATO's Air War for Kosovo: A Strategic and Operational Assessment* (Santa Monica, Calif.: RAND, 2001), pp. 87–88, note 4.

81. See "Army, Taiwan," *Jane's Sentinel Security Assessment: China and Northeast Asia,* 23 April 2007, table, "Air Defense Weapons," available at www.Janes.com.

82. For a description of this system, see "Surface Launched (SL)AMRAAM Complementary Low Altitude Weapon System (CLAWS)," *Defense Update,* www.defense-update.com/products.

83. During the 1982 Falklands War, HMS *Sheffield* was sunk and HMS *Glamorgan* badly damaged by hits by single Exocet ASCMs. The USS *Stark* (FFG 31) nearly sank after being hit by two Iraqi Exocet ASCMs in 1987, and Israel's *Sa'ar*-class corvette *Ahi Hanit* retired from battle after being struck by a Chinese-model C-802 ASCM in 2006. The Exocet and C-802 both have 165 kg (363-pound) warheads.

84. The one exception to this statement is the solitary Lazhou-class LPD, which is equipped with the AK-630 Gatling-gun point-defense system.

85. These radars would be vulnerable to HARM systems, such as Harpy subsonic unmanned drones or China's supersonic KH-31 Krypton missiles. To counter these weapons coastal surveillance radars could be mobile, operated in "blinking" modes from hardened locations, or protected by decoys.

86. Taiwan is developing the 180-mile-range Hsiung Fen III supersonic ASCM; it displayed this weapon during a 13 October 2007 parade.

87. Sofia Wu, "Apache Helicopter Most Suited to Taiwan's Defense Needs: Army," ROC Central News Agency, 10 July 2007, available at www.globalsecurity.org.

88. The MLRS can fire a multitude of rockets with a variety of lethal warheads. Many of these variants could greatly assist Taiwan's defenses, but as presently configured some have ranges that theoretically would allow them to strike China, especially from Penghu. See "MLRS Multiple Launch Rocket System, USA," *Army Technology,* www.army-technology.com/projects.

89. See, for example, Sandra I. Erwin, "Shallow-Water Mines Remain 'Achilles' Heel' of U.S. Navy," *National Defense* (January 2002), available at www.nationaldefensemagazine .org.

90. Commercially available mines can be deployed by two people on the back of a pickup truck. The mines detonate with sufficient force to flip over an amphibious tank.

91. "Army, Taiwan."

92. Cole, *Taiwan's Security,* p. 79.

93. For a careful explanation of other impediments to Taiwan's developing an effective, all-volunteer army, see ibid., pp. 72–90, 102–103.

94. "The biggest unknown is, will they fight?" This is how one retired U.S. military officer who has extensively inspected the Taiwanese army, interviewing both leaders and rank-and-file members, summarized the issue in an interview with the author. See also Cole, *Taiwan's Security,* pp. 88–89.

95. In order to maximize the chances of success, such a campaign would likely be either preceded or accompanied by bombardments designed to destroy the air force and navy, by information warfare, and by decapitation.

96. For example, in 2007 Taiwan had only one LNG terminal, at Yungan, Kaohsiung. Another is being built in Taichung Harbor, with completion slated for 2009. Taiwan has only four oil refineries. See Taiwan Ministry of Energy, "Energy Supply," *The Energy Situation in Taiwan, Republic of China,* www .moeaboe.gov.tw; and U.S. Energy Dept., "Taiwan Country Analysis Brief," *Energy Information Administration,* www.eia.doe.gov.

97. "Taiwan Country Analysis Brief."

98. For example, Taiwan's current crude oil stocks are above ground in vulnerable tank farms. An alternative would be to stockpile refined oil products either underground or in numerous smaller tanks, including indoor tanks at the points of consumption.

99. Substitution, rationing, and cessation of non-essential activities can allow determined blockaded populations to resist for extended periods of time, as numerous historical examples, including Malta and Japan in World War II and Germany in World War I, have shown.

100. E-3 AWACS aircraft, which have 145-foot wingspans and are 144 feet long and 42 feet high, are too large to shelter; see David Shlapak, "Projecting Power in a China-Taiwan Contingency: Implications for USAF and USN Collaboration," in *Coping with the Dragon: Essays on PLA Transformation and the U.S. Military,* ed. Stuart Johnson and Duncan Long (Washington, D.C.: National Defense Univ. Center for Technology and National Security Policy, December 2007),

p. 90, available at www.ndu.edu/ctnsp/pubs/CopingwithDragon.pdf. P-3Cs, which have ninety-eight-foot wingspans and are 115 feet long and thirty-three feet high, may also be too large to shelter.

101. This is one of the fundamental points made by Ted Galen Carpenter in *Let Taiwan Defend Itself,* Cato Policy Analysis 313 (Washington, D.C.: Cato Institute, 24 August 1998), available at www.cato.org/pubs. I agree with much of his analysis and reasoning but disagree on the subject of the United States making available weapons of offensive character.

102. "Joint Communiqué of the United States of America and the People's Republic of China," 17 August 1982, U.S. Information Access program, available at usinfo.state.gov/eap/.